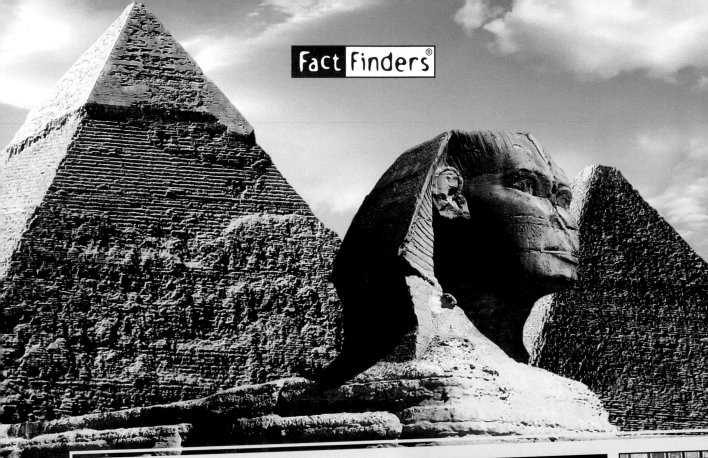

Fact Finders®

GREAT CIVILIZATIONS

# ANCIENT EGYPT

## BEYOND THE PYRAMIDS

by Kathleen W. Deady

CAPSTONE PRESS
a capstone imprint

Fact Finders are published by Capstone Press,
151 Good Counsel Drive, P.O. Box 669, Mankato, Minnesota 56002.
www.capstonepub.com

*Library of Congress Cataloging-in-Publication Data*
Deady, Kathleen W.
 Ancient Egypt : beyond the pyramids / by Kathleen W. Deady.
 p. cm.—(Fact finders. Great civilizations)
 Summary: "Describes ancient Egypt, including its government structure, major achievements,
struggles, and rise to power, as well as its lasting influences on the world"—Provided by publisher.
 Includes bibliographical references and index.
 ISBN 978-1-4296-6830-9 (library binding)
 ISBN 978-1-4296-7235-1 (paperback)
 1. Egypt—Civilization—To 332 B.C.—Juvenile literature. 2. Egypt—History—To 332 B.C.—Juvenile
literature. I. Title. II. Series: Fact finders. Great civilizations.
 DT61.D357 2012
 932.01—dc22                                                                       2010052221

**Editorial Credits**
Carrie Braulick Sheely and Jennifer Besel, editors; Lori Bye, designer; Wanda Winch, media researcher;
   Eric Manske, production specialist

**Photo Credits**
Akg-images: Douglas Macpherson, 5; Alamy: Classic Image, 19; Art Resource, N.Y.: Erich Lessing, 20;
The Bridgeman Art Library International: ©Look and Learn/Private Collection/Fernando Tacconi,
10, ©Look and Learn/Private Collection/Peter Jackson, 23, Russell-Cotes Art Gallery and Museum,
Bournemouth, UK/Frederick Goodall, 9; Dreamstime: Les3photo8, 7 (bottom); Getty Images Inc.:
DEA Picture Library, 7 (top); iStockphoto: robyvannucci, 26; Jupiterimages Corporation, 25 (right);
Shutterstock: Gerard Lazaro 17, (top), Jose Ignacio Soto, cover, 1 (middle right), 25 (left), Kiselev Andrey
Valerevich (hieroglyphs design used as design element), magicinfoto (light beige texture paper design),
Marilyn Volan (grunge paper design), Maugli, cover, 1 (bottom left), Mikhail Zacharnichny, 27, Petrov
Stanislav Eudardovich (parchment paper design), Ramzi Hachicho, cover, 1 (top), sculpies, 17 (bottom),
siloto 28-29 (bottom), Stephen Chung, 15, trappy76, cover, 1 (bottom right); SuperStock: DeAgostini, 13

Printed in the United States of America in Stevens Point, Wisconsin.
032011        006111WZF11

# TABLE OF CONTENTS

# CHAPTER 1

# SECRETS REVEALED

In 1922 **archaeologist** Howard Carter was digging in Egypt's Valley of the Kings. He was looking for King Tutankhamun's tomb in this ancient burial ground. He had been looking for the tomb for many years. Carter knew this might be his last chance to find it.

Eventually, Carter and his workers found stone steps that led to blocked doorways. The last door's seal read "Tutankhamun." Behind the door were four small rooms. Thousands of gold items and jewels filled the rooms. A solid gold coffin held the preserved body, or mummy, of the young king.

King Tutankhamun is known as King Tut. Like other kings of ancient Egypt, he was buried with his clothing, jewelry, and furniture. Ancient Egyptians believed he would need these things in the **afterlife**.

**archaeologist:** a scientist who studies how people lived in the past

**afterlife:** the place where ancient Egyptians believed a person's soul went after death

Two life-size statues stood at the opening to the burial chamber in King Tut's tomb. Scientists think the statues were placed there to guard King Tut's mummy.

**FACT:** A popular story says that King Tut's tomb is cursed. According to the story, people who came in contact with the tomb soon died. This story has been proven false.

King Tut lived in the 1300s BC. He was not an important king. But the discovery of his tomb made him famous. His tomb gave scientists a glimpse of one of the world's great ancient civilizations.

## An Advanced Civilization

The people of ancient Egypt had many new ideas. They were inventors. They studied math, science, and medicine. They also built amazing stone structures, such as pyramids and **obelisks**.

Ancient Egypt was one of the oldest and most advanced civilizations. For 3,000 years, it thrived along the Nile River in northeast Africa.

**obelisk:** a tall stone column with a top shaped like a pyramid

King Tut's tomb held stacks of furniture and other large items.

# Wonderful Things!

When asked if he saw anything while peeking into the tomb, Howard Carter replied, "Yes, wonderful things!" The tomb held thousands of objects. A gold-covered throne and animal-shaped couches were found there. Weapons, board games, paintings, and statues of ancient Egyptian gods were also discovered. A gold burial mask placed on the mummy of King Tut is one of the tomb's most famous items. It took scientists 10 years to record all the tomb's treasures.

King Tut's gold burial mask

# CHAPTER 2

# THE BEGINNINGS OF GREATNESS

The Nile River has always been an important resource for Egyptians. It is one of the few water sources in Egypt's hot, dry land. The Nile River flows from east-central Africa north to the Mediterranean Sea. At 4,160 miles (6,695 kilometers) long, it is the world's longest river.

Around 5,000 years ago, ancient Egyptians began to settle and build permanent homes. Slowly they changed from food gatherers into farmers. They still hunted animals and fished in the Nile. But they also began raising cattle, goats, and sheep. They used these animals for milk and wool.

Ancient Egyptians also began planting seeds in the rich soil of the Nile River valley. They grew wheat, barley, fruits, and vegetables. They wove cloth made from the flax they grew.

Egyptians used water supplied by the Nile River to raise farm animals.

While their farming skills advanced, ancient Egyptians developed other skills. They made farming tools, pottery, baskets, and stone carvings.

**FACT:** The Nile River flooded between June and September. Ancient Egyptians planted crops in October to avoid the flood season.

Ancient Egyptians often used boats to transport goods on the Nile River.

# More Developments

As farming became a way of life, ancient Egyptians continued to advance. They developed a system of **irrigation**. They built boats powered by oars. They also began trading with the nearby kingdoms of Nubia and Mesopotamia.

As settlements grew, leaders organized the communities. Settlements grew into villages, and many villages grew into large towns. Between 3900 and 3100 BC, many towns became wealthy and powerful.

## Upper and Lower Egypt

Eventually, two areas formed into separate kingdoms. Upper Egypt developed in higher parts of the Nile River valley in the south. Lower Egypt grew in the north in the lower **delta** area of the Nile.

The rulers of Upper and Lower Egypt struggled for power over each other. Around 3100 BC, King Narmer of Upper Egypt conquered Lower Egypt. He joined the two lands into one kingdom.

**FACT:** A white crown was a symbol of Upper Egypt. A red crown stood for Lower Egypt.

**irrigation:** a way of bringing water to crops using a system of pipes or channels

**delta:** the area where a river meets the sea; the Nile River splits into many smaller branches to form a delta

# CHAPTER 3

# RISE to POWER

The union of Upper and Lower Egypt started a period of great growth and power for Egypt. A series of strong **dynasties** began ruling the land. More than 30 dynasties held power in ancient Egypt.

## The Early Dynastic Period

The Early Dynastic Period (about 3100–2600 BC) was a time of great achievement. A centralized system of government was one of the most important successes.

King Menes built the center of Egypt's government in Memphis, near present-day Cairo. He was the first king of the First Egyptian Dynasty. The Egyptian king, later called the pharaoh, led the government. The king made the laws. Priests helped the king make decisions as advisors. They held positions such as army commander.

**dynasty:** a series of rulers from the same family

Ancient Egyptians began burying dead rulers near the Nile River at Saqqara during the Early Dynastic Period. Later dynasties continued the practice.

**FACT:** The Egyptians believed their kings were the god Horus in human form.

The central government organized society and improved life for the people. It built a large irrigation system to bring river water to farm fields.

By the First Dynasty, the Egyptians had invented a system of writing. They wrote with pictures called hieroglyphs. Using this written language, Egyptians began keeping careful records for government and important events.

## The Old Kingdom

The Old Kingdom (about 2600–2200 BC) was another time of progress. The government was firmly established and towns grew. Egypt became wealthy and powerful. Ancient Egyptians focused on learning and the arts.

**FACT:** Ancient Egyptians invented the ox-drawn plow as farming developed. The plow helped farmers grow more crops.

Ancient Egyptians often wrote stories in hieroglyphs on tomb and temple walls.

# Leave it to the Experts!

Hieroglyphic writing was difficult to learn. The signs could stand for one sound, more than one sound, a whole word, or an idea. Most Egyptians could not write hieroglyphs. Professional writers called scribes studied for years to learn more than 700 signs. Scribes were important to the kings. They wrote tax and court records as well as other important reports.

The Third Dynasty's second king, Djoser, had a chief scribe called Imhotep. Imhotep was a talented **architect**. He built the Step Pyramid of Saqqara for King Djoser's tomb. It was one of the first stone buildings in the world. The pyramid was also the largest building of its time.

The Egyptians later built even bigger pyramids. These pyramids were built for the tombs of other Old Kingdom rulers. King Snofru ruled during the Fourth Dynasty from about 2613 to 2589 BC. During his rule, three pyramids were built.

Around 2560 BC, Egyptians built the Great Pyramid of Giza during the rule of Snofru's son, King Khufu. This pyramid was made of more than 2.5 million limestone blocks. The Great Pyramid is Ancient Egypt's largest pyramid. Its base covers 13 acres (5.3 hectares), and it stands about 450 feet (137 m) tall.

Egyptians built two more large pyramids at Giza. These pyramids were built for Khufu's son and grandson. Egyptians also built a huge statue called the Great Sphinx at Giza. Most historians believe it was built to guard the pyramids.

**architect:** a person who designs buildings

The Step Pyramid stood 204 feet (62 m) tall after it was built.

The Giza pyramids are regularly restored to help keep them from wearing down over time.

**FACT:** The Old Kingdom is also known as the Pyramid Age.

# CHAPTER 4

# UPS AND DOWNS

King Pepi II ruled during the Sixth Dynasty. The rule of Pepi II was the longest in Egyptian history. He ruled for about 94 years.

Near the end of the Sixth Dynasty, local rulers and priests started fighting each other for power. The king's power weakened. Around 2134 BC, Egypt broke into separate states. These states lasted about 100 years.

The Seventh to Tenth Dynasties ruled Egypt in the First Intermediate Period (about 2150–2000 BC). Rulers during this period faced many troubles. People neglected the irrigation systems. Poor harvests caused a lack of food. Thieves broke into pyramids. The First Intermediate Period came to an end in about 2040 BC. After years of struggle, rulers in the city of Thebes united the kingdom again.

**FACT:** According to records, King Pepi II became pharaoh at age 6.

When thieves robbed tombs, they often broke valuable items and left the tombs in shambles.

## The Middle Kingdom

King Mentuhotep gained control of Egypt after the First Intermediate Period. He moved the capital to Thebes. With a strong central government, Egypt began to recover as the Middle Kingdom (about 2000–1800 BC) began.

King Mentuhotep worked to rebuild the kingdom. He expanded Egypt's territory and traded with other kingdoms. He also repaired and improved irrigation systems.

In 1991 BC, King Amenemhet began the Twelfth Dynasty. During this dynasty, Egypt became wealthy and powerful again. Egypt again conquered Nubian lands and built up trade with Palestine and Syria.

Asian invaders called Hyksos came to Egypt around 1800 BC. As their numbers grew, so did their power. They took control of Egypt around 1640 BC. Hyksos kings ruled for about 100 years. The Hyksos taught Egyptians how to make bronze weapons and **chariots** for war.

Around 1550 BC, the Egyptians defeated the Hyksos. General Ahmose drove the Hyksos out of Egypt, and he became king. Ahmose's rule began the New Kingdom (about 1570–1100 BC).

bronze dagger
from ancient Egypt

**chariot:** a two-wheeled fighting platform that was usually pulled by horses

# Growth of Ancient Egypt

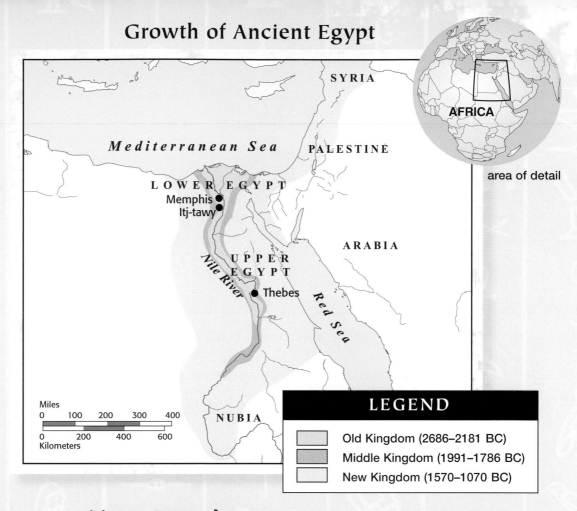

SYRIA

AFRICA

area of detail

*Mediterranean Sea*

PALESTINE

L O W E R  E G Y P T

Memphis

Itj-tawy

*Nile River*

U P P E R
E G Y P T

Thebes

ARABIA

*Red Sea*

NUBIA

Miles
0   100   200   300   400

0      200      400      600
Kilometers

## LEGEND

Old Kingdom (2686–2181 BC)
Middle Kingdom (1991–1786 BC)
New Kingdom (1570–1070 BC)

# New Kingdom

Under King Ahmose, the Egyptians worked so they would never be overrun again. Egypt built a strong army. King Thutmose I later used the army to take control of land in Syria and Palestine.

During the New Kingdom, Ancient Egyptians buried their rulers in the Valley of the Kings near Thebes. These tombs were cut into the sides of hills. The tombs were easier to guard than the pyramids.

21

# CHAPTER 5

# GONE BUT NOT FORGOTTEN

At the end of the New Kingdom, Egypt's central power grew weak. Pharaohs slowly lost control over lands outside Egypt. Alexander the Great of Macedonia conquered Egypt in 332 BC. For more than 300 years, Macedonian Greeks ruled Egypt.

In 30 BC, the Romans defeated the Egyptian navy at the Battle of Actium. Egypt then became part of the Roman Empire.

But the ancient Egyptian culture is far from lost. From buildings to weapons, ancient Egyptians left much behind for scientists to study.

**FACT:** Workers used barrels to help them build the pyramids. They counted the number of times a barrel turned and used it as a measurement for length.

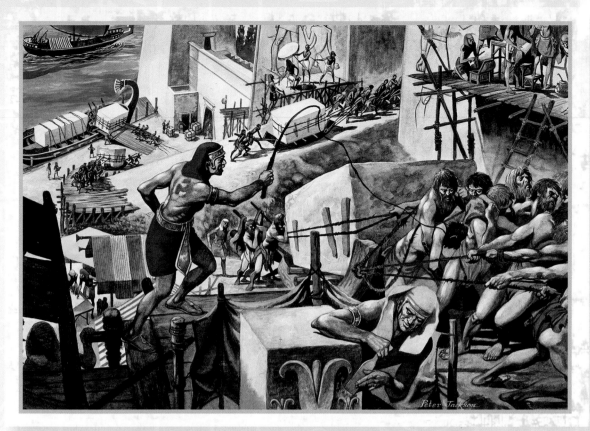

Some blocks used for ancient Egyptian pyramids weighed about 2 tons (1.8 metric tons).

## Pyramids and Other Tombs

The pyramids are Egypt's best-known achievement. They are the oldest large stone structures in the world. It's easy to see why people are still amazed by them. Historians believe the grueling job of building just one pyramid took about 20 years. Workers cut stone blocks from rock. Slaves dragged the blocks to boats. The boats floated down the Nile to the building site. Slaves hauled the stone blocks up ramps to place on a pyramid.

The tombs of ancient Egyptian kings are important discoveries. Egyptians decorated the walls of their tombs with artwork. The paintings show ancient Egyptians' religious beliefs and everyday activities. Weapons, tools, furniture, and other items from tombs also teach scientists about everyday life in Ancient Egypt.

## Hieroglyphs

Ancient Egyptians left behind many written records. These records appear on the walls of temples and tombs, **papyrus** rolls, stone slabs, and pottery.

By AD 500, Egyptians no longer used hieroglyphs. They began to use a simpler alphabet that they learned from the Greeks. Egyptians quickly forgot how to read and write in their ancient language. For hundreds of years, hieroglyphs remained a mystery.

Then in 1799, someone found a rock slab outside of Rosetta, Egypt. The slab, called the Rosetta Stone, contained Greek writing and two forms of Egyptian writing.

**FACT:** The modern decimal system is based on ancient Egyptian math.

Ancient Egyptian artwork often shows gods with humanlike bodies and heads in the form of animals.

Ancient Egyptian priests wrote the text on the Rosetta Stone in 196 BC.

Jean-Francois Champollion, a French scholar, compared words he knew in Greek to words in hieroglyphs. In 1822 he figured out the meaning of the hieroglyphs. The world could at last understand what the ancient Egyptians had written.

**papyrus:** a tall water plant that grows along the Nile River

# Mummies

Mummies also unlock mysteries of ancient Egypt. Ancient Egyptians believed that preserving the dead helped prepare them for the afterlife. The Egyptians' mummification process involved many steps. Their careful work helped some mummies last until modern times.

Mummies help scientists learn more about ancient Egyptians. Scientists can tell what ancient Egyptians ate and what diseases they had. King Tut's mummy has been studied many times. Scientists think he may have died of malaria. This serious disease is carried by mosquitoes.

# Calendar Records

Ancient Egyptians studied **astronomy** and tracked repeating events, such as the flooding of the Nile. From this knowledge, they made a 365-day calendar that they used to record events. These calendars have helped historians learn when things happened in Ancient Egypt.

During mummification, ancient Egyptians placed most of a body's organs in jars.

**astronomy:** the study of stars, planets, and other objects in space

Ancient Egyptian mummies are displayed in museums around the world.

## Lasting Influences

Ancient Egyptians influenced the world in many ways. They made advances in science, math, and agriculture. Ancient Egyptian influence on architecture can be seen in many buildings around the world. Scientists continue making discoveries in Egypt. They hope to uncover even more secrets of this great civilization.

**FACT:** In 2010 scientists found tombs with mummies south of Cairo, Egypt. Scientists think some of the tombs are more than 4,500 years old.

# TIMELINE

**5000–3900 BC**

Early people settle around the Nile River, grow crops, and develop farming communities.

**2040 BC**

King Mentuhotep gains control of Egypt and moves the capital to Thebes.

**1640 BC**

Hyksos seize power and occupy Egypt until about 1550.

**5000**　　**3000**　　　　**2000**　　　　　**1600**

**3100 BC**

King Narmer unites Upper and Lower Egypt.

**2134–2040 BC**

Egypt breaks into separate states.

## 1550 BC

General Ahmose drives the Hyksos from Egypt and becomes king; he begins making Egypt a strong military power.

## 332 BC

Alexander the Great from Macedonia conquers Egypt.

## 30 BC

The Romans defeat the Egyptian navy at the Battle of Actium; Egypt becomes part of the Roman Empire.

**1500**  **1000**  **300**  **30**

## 712–332 BC

Rulers from Nubia, Assyria, and Persia govern Egypt.

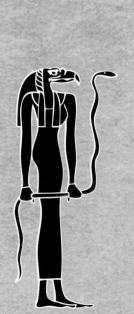

29

# GLOSSARY

**afterlife** (AF-tur-life)—the place where Egyptians believed a person's soul went after death

**archaeologist** (ar-kee-OL-uh-jist)—a scientist who studies how people lived in the past

**architect** (AR-kuh-tekt)—a person who designs buildings

**astronomy** (uh-STRAH-nuh-mee)—the study of stars, planets, and other objects in space

**chariot** (CHAYR-ee-uht)—a two-wheeled fighting platform used in ancient times that was usually pulled by horses

**delta** (DEL-tuh)—the area where a river meets the sea; the Nile River splits into many smaller branches to form a delta

**dynasty** (DYE-nuh-stee)—a series of rulers from the same family; the oldest son of a king's first wife usually took over as king

**irrigation** (ihr-uh-GAY-shuhn)—a way of bringing water to crops using a system of pipes or channels

**obelisk** (OB-uh-lisk)—a tall stone column with a top shaped like a pyramid

**papyrus** (puh-PYE-ruhss)—a tall water plant that grows along the Nile River; paper can be made from the stems of this plant

# READ MORE

**Corrick, James A.** *Gritty, Stinky Ancient Egypt: The Disgusting Details about Life in Ancient Egypt.* Disgusting History. Mankato, Minn.: Capstone Press, 2011.

**MacDonald, Fiona.** *Solving the Mysteries of the Pyramids.* Digging into History. New York: Marshall Cavendish Benchmark, 2009.

**Malam, John.** *The Egyptians.* Dig It: History from Objects. New York: PowerKids Press, 2011.

# INTERNET SITES

FactHound offers a safe, fun way to find Internet sites related to this book. All of the sites on FactHound have been researched by our staff.

Here's all you do:

Visit *www.facthound.com*

Type in this code: 9781429668309

Super-cool stuff! Check out projects, games and lots more at **www.capstonekids.com**

# INDEX